for Oonagh

First published 1989 as *The Little Dog Laughed* by Macmillan Children's Books
This edition published 2000 by Macmillan Children's Books
a division of Macmillan Publishers Limited
20 New Wharf Road, London N1 9RR
Basingstoke and Oxford
Associated companies throughout the world
www.panmacmillan.com

ISBN: 978-0-333-78104-3

Text and illustrations copyright © Lucy Cousins 1989, 1998 and 2000
Moral rights asserted.

9 8

A CIP catalogue record for this book is available from the British Library.

Printed in China

Lucy Cousins'
book of
Nursery
rhymes

MACMILLAN CHILDREN'S BOOKS

Contents

Jack and Jill 6

Jack be nimble 8

I had a little nut tree 9

One, two, buckle my shoe 10

Humpty Dumpty 12

Sing a song of sixpence 14

Old Mother Hubbard 16

Little Miss Muffet 17

The lion and the unicorn 18

Mary, Mary, quite contrary 20

Polly put the kettle on 21

Oh, the brave old Duke of York 22

Mary had a little lamb 24

Rub-a-dub-dub 25

The Queen of Hearts 26

One, two, three, four 28

Tom, Tom, the piper's son 29

Wee Willie Winkie 30

Jack and Jill
Went up the hill
To fetch a pail of water.
Jack fell down
And broke his crown,
And Jill came tumbling after.

Then up Jack got
And home did trot
As fast as he could caper.
To old Dame Frown,
Who patched up his crown
With vinegar and brown paper.

Jack be nimble,
Jack be quick,
Jack jump over
The candlestick.

I had a little nut tree,
Nothing would it bear
But a silver nutmeg
And a golden pear.

The King of Spain's daughter
Came to visit me,
And all for the sake
Of my little nut tree.

One, two, buckle my shoe;

Three, four, knock at the door;

Five, six, pick up sticks;

Seven, eight, lay them straight;

Nine, ten, a big fat hen;

Eleven, twelve, dig and delve;

Thirteen, fourteen, maids a-courting;

Fifteen, sixteen, maids in the kitchen;

Seventeen, eighteen, maids in waiting;

Nineteen, twenty, my plate's empty.

humpty dumpty sat on a Wall

Humpty Dumpty
Sat on a wall.
Humpty Dumpty
Had a great fall.
All the King's horses
And all the King's men
Couldn't put Humpty
Together again.

Sing a song of sixpence,
A pocket full of rye,
Four and twenty blackbirds
Baked in a pie.

When the pie was opened,
The birds began to sing.
Wasn't that a dainty dish
To set before the King?

old mother hubbard

Old Mother Hubbard
Went to the cupboard
To fetch her poor dog a bone.
But when she got there,
The cupboard was bare,
And so the poor dog had none.

The dame made a curtsy,
The dog made a bow.
The dame said, your servant.
The dog said, bow-wow.

bow
wow

little
miss
muffet

Little Miss Muffet sat on a tuffet,

Eating her curds and whey.

Then along came a spider

Who sat down beside her

And frightened Miss Muffet away.

the lion
and the
unicorn

The lion and the unicorn
Were fighting for the crown.
The lion beat the unicorn
All around the town.

Some gave them white bread,
And some gave them brown.
Some gave them plum cake
And drummed them out of town.

Mary, Mary, quite contrary,
How does your garden grow?
With silver bells and cockleshells,
And pretty maids all in a row.

mary mary

Polly put the kettle on,
Polly put the kettle on,
Polly put the kettle on,
We'll all have tea.

Sukey take it off again,
Sukey take it off again,
Sukey take it off again,
They've all gone away.

Oh, the brave old Duke of York,
He had ten thousand men.
He marched them up to the top of the hill,
And he marched them down again.

And when they were up, they were up,
And when they were down, they were down,
And when they were only halfway up,
They were neither up nor down.

the brave old duke of York

mary had a little lamb

Mary had a little lamb,
Its fleece was white as snow.
And everywhere that Mary went
The lamb was sure to go.

It followed her to school one day,
That was against the rule.
It made the children laugh and play
To see a lamb at school.

rub-a-dub-dub

Rub-a-dub-dub, three men in a tub,

And how do you think they got there?

The butcher, the baker, the candlestick-maker,

They all jumped out of a rotten potato.

'Twas enough to make a man stare.

The Queen of Hearts
She made some tarts,
All on a summer's day.
The Knave of Hearts
He stole those tarts
And took them clean away.

The King of Hearts
Called for the tarts
And beat the Knave full sore.
The Knave of Hearts
Brought back the tarts
And vowed he'd steal no more.

the Queen of hearts she made some tarts

One, two, three, four,
Mary at the cottage door,
Five, six, seven, eight,
Eating cherries off a plate.

Tom, Tom, the piper's son

Tom, Tom, the piper's son,

Stole a pig and away did run.

The pig was eat,

And Tom was beat,

And Tom went howling down the street.

Wee Willie Winkie
Runs through the town,
Upstairs and downstairs
In his nightgown,
Rapping at the window,
Crying through the lock,
"Are the children in their beds?
For now it's eight o'clock."